LOVE
WORDS
AND WINE

Cleo Selena

LOVE WORDS AND WINE

ISBN: 978-1-7391000-2-5

Cleo Selena
cleoselena.com
@lovewordsandwine

for women everywhere who have suffered in their loneliness.
you will survive.

POEMS

i haven't told myself recently
that i love you.
you are magnificent—
a woman of strength
and so much power,
even if you don't feel it
in this exact moment.
your love and magnetism
are always within you.
you can sparkle again.
everything you need is inside,
inside that glorious body,
deep within your organs—
so today you can stay calm,
resist the urge,
and release control.
i love, forgive, and will honour you
every single day of the week.

with a kiss from the moon,
she made a wish
that all her desires
would fly through the sky,
engulfing her in a warm embrace.
life is going to go
just her way.

i have never believed in karma,
but if I did,
I must have done something
really fucking bad
to have the year i've had.

there's still two months left, too.
maybe I will heal.
maybe I will walk.
i hope he will love me.

come on, year . . .
it's time to turn things around.

it's time to stop white-knuckling it.
allow some space for the magic to flow
and release all of your expectations
as the world is here to support you.
it's more imaginative than you know.
reduce your grip on others
as you know only good things are coming.

taking a walk on a monday
is the best start to the week:
getting those steps in,
feeling the breeze on my arms,
and taking time away.
it's good to take a minute.
enjoy the gardens and
see the butterflies.
it's a way to feel grounded,
and you only have to
step through the door.

that hug felt so good.
inside your warm embrace,
snuggled within you–
i wanted to stay there forever,
or at least a little longer.
your heartbeat against mine:
a feeling of total comfort.

seeing your face,
your beautiful eyes,
and your handsome looks
on that app
broke my heart.
even though it's not wrong,
it doesn't feel right
for either of us to be there.
let's forget those who swiped
and spend time with each other.
i'd rather have your touch
than to hold a phone.

i imagine what you're doing:
lying in your bed,
your head on a soft pillow
as you close your brown eyes.
i hope you think of me
even if it's for a moment.
I send you so much love
from my heart to yours.

at 4 o'clock they said
you took your last breath
here on earth.
what a sad moment.
i hope you were at peace
and no longer in pain.
i will miss your kindness
and your laugh,
but i hope you are reunited
with those loved ones
who also left too soon–
that they are giving you a hug
and smiling down at our tears.
it happened so quickly,
which is why it's such a surprise
but I will remember every moment
with happiness, fondness, and a smile.

it feels so strange and
so empty to know
that i will never see you–
at least not earthside.
i am glad you're not in pain,
but it still feels like a void.
you told me grief is selfish
and i agree,
but never seeing someone again
hurts like hell.
i pray there's a heaven
and you're reunited with
those who already left us.

i bet there will be plenty of hugs.

it's time to not give a fuck
and to show up in the most
fabulous and unapologetic way.
get out there and be iconic
there's nothing to lose
and so much to gain.

peace and love
in the world,
in the heart,
in the mind.
peace and love
are what's needed
for you
and for me.
peace and love
feels so good.
it's time to release
and let it all go.

i've been thinking about the future . . .
i hope you will be in mine,
and i smile thinking of being part of yours:
the fun we can have making plans,
bringing joy to each other's lives,
not worried when we are apart
and embracing the times we are together.
let's hope it's not too much longer
until we are enclosed in each other's arms.

13

a room full of white flowers
and love–
i have to admit
it hurt a little,
but it was an honour
to see the union
a new mr.
and mrs.
a day of love,
friendship, and dancing.

at one point today,
it felt like one of the worse days
i've ever experienced,
but by the end
i just couldn't give any more fucks.
i said what I said
and am putting my magnetic energy in a different place.
i know we will return together at some point,
maybe in a few days
or in a few weeks,
but for now I am directing my feminine energy
into my creativity.

tonight I felt relaxed,
like a weight has been lifted.
i don't know how long it's here
but i would like for it to last.
it doesn't mean i don't crave you.
i still miss your love and touch,
but it does mean i feel peace—
peace today and more tomorrow.
i believe we will reconnect,
but for now i close my eyes,
take a deep breath,
and remember the good times
because i am thankful for those.

today i thought i was fine
until the clock struck midnight.
then the tears came flooding.
i saw you untagged your life,
removed it from mine,
and that hurt so much.
i can't wait for you to be proud again
and for the day we snuggle together.
i know you will share our photos
because together we are an
incredible couple of people.
i miss you now but I know
you will come back again
so we can rebuild,
have fun,
and love again.

it feels so exciting to fall back in love
and to do it together day by day,
a small piece of the heart at a time.
i can't wait to be held and
for you to lean in and kiss me again.
it will feel so nice,
so tingly in my body.
it will be a moment we cherish
in both our bodies for a long time.

love that's real,
love that's whole,
love that's pure.

that wasn't meant to happen—
i had been doing so well,
but the thought of two dates
threw me to the floor.
to think of you with others
when we could be working on ourselves
feels so unfair,
like the world is tilted,
and I am struggling to hold on as the waves hit.
I know in my heart that we will be together one day.
but tonight, for a moment,
my confidence was shaken.

I can't wait to once again be
the lucky girl on a date with you.

today felt like a good day.
the only thing missing
was a touch and a kiss,
but I can be patient
and wait for what's to come.
it felt good to spend time
in each other's company.
i will treasure this feeling
until it is real once again.

sitting in my room, listening to old love songs
reminds me of a simpler time many years ago.
i saw a photo of you yesterday
and felt nothing,
but it has been forever.
so much has happened since we last spoke,
including you having a little girl who is so cute.
life has changed so much since playing cricket
and touring Scotland.
they were good moments,
a snippet of life away from
prying eyes and the land down under.
take me back so we can do it all again,
almost all–
you know the bit I would change.
what a time we had.

as the waves splash
up and down and up again,
the boat holds on,
thrashed around, bobbing
up and down and down again.
if you hold on tight,
you will go back up
and the one you love
will be there to catch you.

heavy eyes
and a weary mind—
close them tight.
you are safe.
dream of love,
of joy, and of happiness.
stop being scared.
just shut your eyes.

i know there are men who want me–
it feels so good to close my eyes
and picture all of them around me.
it's nice to have it and soak them in.
i see you standing there, too,
with your eyes wide, looking up with pride
your arms wide open, ready to hug me,
to share your commitment and love with me.
it feels fun to know there are other men
but better knowing you want me.

you bastard.
why are you doing this?
forget her now.
this is stupid–
come back to me,
the one you love.

i saw so many white feathers
whilst i was out walking.
they let me know that everything
will be okay and that my
loved ones are telling me so.
i saw so many white feathers
that i couldn't help but smile.
it feels good to know
that they are there
watching over me and
letting me know it will all be okay.
it will all turn out exactly how I want it to.

this weekend has been hard.
i've missed you so much.
the message from you today
felt so good, even if it was
only chores you mentioned,
but then i craved more.
i resisted taking action
as you want your space.
it was hard but i survived.
i know that you will come.
for today i had to be
grateful for the messages.

whether it's the
moon or the sun
or the stars above
who are leading
the way,
one day i know
they will pull me
all the way back,
right into your arms,
your embrace, and
your everlasting love.

it's the waiting which is the worst part,
but at the same time,
i don't want the day to arrive yet.

a time to say goodbye,
which is something
i am not ready for,
not quite yet.

i know you'll be looking down
smiling and sending love.

lights in the night sky
flicker and fizz,
sending waves into the body,
pushing out the bad,
and asking in the better–
giving more love and fun
and abundance and joy.
oh yes! the lights shine
and so do you, now,
every single day.

life in the big city;
it's crowded, crazy, and fun.
different accents float in the air
as people talk and move
on to the next destination of choice.
so many happy memories
of being there with you . . .
can we make some new ones soon?

our dear girl,
let's hope we made you proud
and that you were wiping our tears
from your new place up in the sky,
wondering why we were making a fuss

but feeling warmth because we all came out
just for you.
you will be so so missed.
let's hope you can keep watching over us all
every single day.

grief, laughter, heartbreak
all at once, all entwined,
one at a time,
piece by piece.
you can pick yourself up.
things will get better.
you can laugh more,
remember the good times,
and maybe even have
life together again.

yesterday was a nice surprise–
to watch a film and talk away.
today, i miss you a lot.
i feel like i'm meant to be strong,
not show emotions,
and not reach out.
that doesn't make it easier,
but i am giving you space,
room to miss me and then
to get back to loving me.

. . . and there's only love and light
as the darkness lifts.
dreaming of your arms around me
makes me feel more lonely.
the cold and the rain–
i don't like it here.
let me out of the dark.
we wait for the clocks to shift
as the night draws in.
it is darkness.

the future sounds crazy,
but i have a feeling
it will all be ok:
full of fizz, sparkle,
joy, laughter, and sex
what a great future that would be.
i can't wait for all of those experiences.

i really miss you right now
in this moment
as i sit on our bed.
the only comfort is that
i know you miss me too.
you miss me even more.
you desire me.
you want me.
you dream about me.

i am a million-pound woman,
i am a writer,
i am a businesswoman
with the man I most desire
right here by my side.
i am strong,
i am great,
i am always the best.
he came back and fell to my feet
to declare his love . . . *i love you.*
as i grew in confidence,
my heart pounded and the pain left.
we are back together,
building the life and the love
that i have always deserved.
i am so powerful.
i radiate magnetism wherever I go.
he can't get enough of me.
my life is full of abundance
and sparkly knee-high boots.
my body is strong–
i am sexy and magnetic.
everybody loves me,
especially him.
he dreams about me tonight.
i am changing the world
though my words
and my thoughts.
i am always the one.
i am always chosen.
i am always loved.
i am taking up space
without any apology.
he loves me more every day.
we are together now
and never apart again.

of course he wants to spend time with me.
i am beautiful and wonderful to be around every single day.
i am always his main priority and he hates being away from me.
i am the best choice and he has no doubt about it.
i am the woman of his dreams. he is thinking of me.
the past has happened but that won't stop our future:
a future where we are back together,
having the most incredible and expressive sex,
and being our best selves together.
it's inevitable to desire each other
and create a relationship a million times better
than the one we had before.

as we sat across from each other
in the candle-lit restaurant,
his hand brushed mine
and my stomach flipped.
it felt like the first time—
no, it was better than that.
he gently held my hand,
his soft skin against mine.
he looked deep into my eyes,
looking at me like he could see
my beating heart.
he could see how fast
the rush of red was flowing around my body,
i want to be with you,
he whispered, so sincere
and with absolute certainty
i replied *i believe you.*

my phone beeps.
it's him–
of course it is.
he is obsessed,
can never stop talking.
i don't blame him.
he loves me,
he misses me,
he wants me–
what a lucky guy he is.

did you know i am empowered?
yes indeed.
it feels so good
and i know you can see it.
i am fucking beautiful–
that is clear.
the world can see it.

i can now get what i want.
i can now do what i want.
i can now have some fun.

don't be boring as hell,
be sexy as fuck.
radiate all of who you are.
be your truest self.
show the world
your best version.
be radiant now.
they will always see you shine.

no more tears,
no more sadness,
no more frustration.

only more joy,
only more fun,
only more sex.

just me,
just him.

it finally happened last night.
that moment was more magical
than it had ever been before.
your lips against mine,
all of your body hard to me.
we may have been here in the past,
but it's different now.
we never will never be apart again.

in my darkest moments,
i still thought of you.
in my happiest times,
i still thought of you.
on the sad days,
i still thought of you.
in the best hours,
i still thought of you.

it all turns out even better
than you could ever imagine;
the man of your dreams,
the wealth you deserve,
the body you desire–
you have it all
and it feels so good.

it's not fake,
our love together.
it's a real hit-you-in-the-balls,
extraordinary love.
i know you feel it.
now and always,
this is forever.

love is a feeling of contentment–
the way you look at me
and don't even realise it.
it's understanding each other,
even on a rainy day.
but most of all
it's you and me,
together now and always
because we are love.

although i've known you forever,
our new journey is beginning now.
it's different and that's okay.
in fact, it's even better now.
you had to see the grass isn't greener.
it was a chance for me to heal.
now our love is even greater.
our happiness cemented forever.
it's you and me and that's all we need.

i love you every night.
i talk to you every night.
i touch you every night.
i hold you every night.

my dreams are open to you—
step inside and sleep tight.

you want me.
you need me.
you see me.
you love me.

i am ready for you.
now is the time.

Printed in Great Britain
by Amazon

28284255R00064

i am enough.
being a woman
makes me this way.
you are enough.
being a woman
makes you this way.
let's show the word
that we are
more than enough.

it didn't matter how dark it got.
the light always shone though–
only a little bit on some days,
but the days i saw you?
those days were the brightest
even if it didn't seem it.
now that we are back in each other's arms,
every single day shines so brightly.
any darker day will be ok
now that you're here to share it.

you ran back to me.
i didn't expect it
on that specific day
even though i had dreamed
that i would feel your touch
again at some point.
it was better than i hoped–
your wish fulfilled.

i am a self-fulfilling prophecy.
i knew you would come back.
you are here with me now.
i said it, i wished for you,
and now we are together.
i got my love back
and you are even better than before.

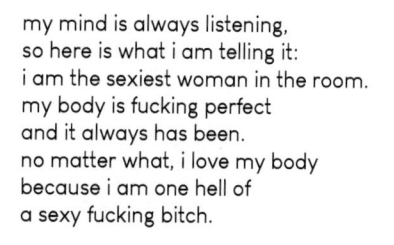

my mind is always listening,
so here is what i am telling it:
i am the sexiest woman in the room.
my body is fucking perfect
and it always has been.
no matter what, i love my body
because i am one hell of
a sexy fucking bitch.

this is the new version of you:
the one who believes in herself
and who loves everything about herself.
you are the woman who lights up the room
and gets all of her lifes desires.
you are irresistible to everyone
and no one ever forgets you.
it's time to go for it.
you won't believe how good it feels.

i trust you.

59

here i fucking go.
i am the woman who gets it.
i always get what i want.
worthiness is within me,
and it's inside of you too.

spoiler alert, it all gets good.
you get everything you are dreaming of
and more, so much more.
your soulmate comes back.
and he could never get you
out of his head.
love is better together than it ever has been.
it's strong, it's fun, it's trusting.
he can never take his eyes off you.
the love you have for each other is intense.
you are in a bubble of love
and it's so very perfect.
you sell your books
and you are a huge business success–
everything you touch turns to gold.
every few months, you travel with joy.
there are so many memories made
and there's a little girl who loves to hold your hands.
you finally love your body;
it's even more perfect than before.
love and abundance shine through.
every day is filled with joy.
you have it all. everything you wish for
is already here and it's so so good.

19

the tears flowed too much.
my worst thoughts came alive.
abandoned,
left behind without looking back.
i wish i'd have had said more.
maybe it would have happened sooner.
i'm glad i stayed quiet for longer.
it gave us more memories,
and some were still good.
time has gone by now
and i miss you, how i miss you.
the bond we have together–
i know you'll never find it again.
i feel you pulling forward,
slowly right now, but this time
i know you will be back
for i am your shining light,
and when we join together again,
we will never make the same mistakes.
your love for me is so deep.
it's ready to grow.
the sun will shine again for us.
i am so excited for that moment:
a precious point together
like two diamonds kissing.

it was a floppy dick with her
no matter how much you tried
with booze, pills, and porn.
you know why?
because she is not me.
i am the only one who makes you hard,
of course i am.
and you can see that now.
ready to get stiff again?
then you know where our bed is.

everything hurts me.
i love being sensitive.
it makes me wildly great.
i feel so deeply
and now i own it.

i'm here thinking about you–
sitting in the home we share,
but you are not here.
it's ok to remember the good times,
the laughter we had,
the kisses,
and all of those hugs.
i am no longer dwelling.
we both could have behaved
very differently.
i know in every cell of my body
that you miss me.
so while i'm thinking about you,
i can feel you dreaming of me.

i'm writing again.
i've taken it back.
it's here in this notebook.
i'm using words of expression
i trust are mine.
i've unlocked the door
and i will not stop.

for a second i froze,
wondering if it's true,
but then i smelt him.
he is still here,
still home,
and forever with me.

listen to women:
we have a voice
loud and uncompromising
like a rocket launching.
with more women
at the top of the galaxy,
our world would be inspired
for women hold kindness.
it's time to be heard.

i came to burn it to the fucking ground,
leaving only the ash behind.
the fire was lit inside my heart
but then i paused for a second.
i don't want to destroy it.
that won't erase the memories.
instead, it's time to rebuild
from the inside to the outer corners.
i am here and ready whenever it's right.

cataclysmic heartbreak drove her
down into the darkest parts of her heart,
into a pain she didn't realise could exist,
until there was a moment
when she realised she couldn't go on.
living like this was no life—
like a hermit snuggled under the sheets.
she was so sick of herself
that she had to write.
words pouring out of her into her fingers
and dancing naked in the hallway—
the little things brought her back.
it was at this period of her day
when he returned full of sorrow,
and despite the hurt and torment,
she opened her arms and her heart again,
knowing there would be no more pain
and that if there was,
she would survive.

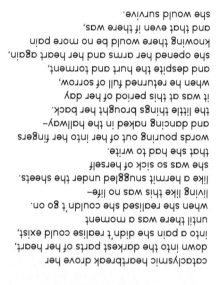

let's celebrate love forever
because it feels so good,
like a bee finding its nectar.
it feels like home
when it's you and me.
let's celebrate love forever,
no matter what's happening today.
there is no more incredible feeling
than to love and be loved,
especially when it's between us.

you just keep going.
i know you won't stop.
you have big things to do.
those feelings in your heart
that you can not shake
are there for a reason.
even if you can't see them,
never let them go.
the whole world needs you,
so put one foot forward
and fulfil your purpose.

they say her heart didn't burn
even though her whole world did.
that beating heart of hers
stayed strong and always believed.
it believed love would come back to it.
it knew he would be home soon
and they could rebuild from the ashes.

never let anyone burn your love.

joan was going to save france
and she was going to save herself.
no white horse is needed,
instead only love and belief
to put back together the smashed pieces.
it might not be as heroic,
but it will save her life.
she will be complete again
and come through the battle
even stronger than before.

i noticed someone else.
for years i kept my head down,
eyes focused on only you.
lately, i've realised there's more.
it's not that i don't want you–
i'd love that more than anything.
i can't wait for my heart to beat,
feeling your touch on my body,
warm hands soft on my skin.
for now, i'm putting myself up
high on the pedestal
instead of hiding behind a bookcase.
anyone and everyone
owes love to me now.
when you love me again,
i will keep noticing
and my eyes will never fall
because i am worthy of love
from you and the rest of the world.

he loves me
truly, madly, deeply.
i am his whole world.
we can't stop—
he will never stop—
he doesn't want to stop.
every day he thinks of me,
each night, too.
i live in his head
and he loves it
as he desires me
all of me. now.

i lost the weight,
i made the money,
he came back.
life is good and
the world is great.

i am tipsy in love
and it feels so good–
two hearts beating together,
a kiss which ignites.
everything inside is excited.
love is the best gift.
we have it now
and i'm not letting it go.

the best lovers are fighters.
we go hard for what we believe,
never letting go of what we want,
what we are passionate about
in love, in art, in life.
we can be scrappy
and our emotions take over.
it's because we care,
we want what we desire,
and will never be stopped.
we will go to battle for our needs
to make sure we get what we deserve.
we are ready to go right now.

you love it when i am firey
and when i cry hard.
you love it when i act a bit cuckoo
when i get mad.
you love it when i tell you i love you
when i share my heart.
you love it when i am ridiculous
when i show i care.

be careful what you wish for—
my guy is obsessed with me.
he is always looking at me,
he is always touching me,
he is always talking to me,
and the sex?
hey, that's between us.
it's all happening
exactly how i hoped.

it's time to take up space
and make room for me
as i am finally ready
to be seen
and heard.
you won't miss me
for i am taking up the full capacity.

the truth is that the love of my life
is sleeping on the sofa
whilst his new woman
thinks he has his own bedroom.
we walk around naked
and he buys me beautiful flowers.
i know we will be together again
very, very soon.
it's what i desire,
and i am a magnificent female.
i can see that despite everything,
he still loves me too.

everything we see is a lie—
the instagram posts,
the new happiness,
the fake selfies,
and your pretend life.

icons do whatever the fuck they want.
it's time to live the most iconic life.
be like liz and marry dick again.
push through all that fear
and finally drive your own life.
take up all the room you need.
blaze bright and expand your aura.
there's nothing bigger than regret,
so step out of your way
and do something unpredictable.
go create your own path.

84

she wore red lipstick to the coffee shop
and the world took notice.
she wore a low-cut top to the supermarket
and the world took notice.
she cut her hair short
and the world took notice.
she did whatever the fuck she wanted
because she could.
it was her time to take up all the space.

it's time to die
for i'm ready to rebirth–
to be indestructible
and lose all the unneeded parts of me
that keep me small
and which bring tears.
i don't need them now
for i am magnificent.

the last time i had sex with him
was in an airport hotel.
i thought we would work things out.
i expected to fix it fast.
if i'd known, i would have taken it slower—
felt him with me for longer.
it could have been even better.
i want to do it again now.
writing this makes me crave him.
we will have it again soon
and when we do, it will be
the best time of his life.

what i do today
creates my tomorrow.
i'm giving myself love, joy,
lots of happiness,
and a radiating smile.
i'm giving myself the man of my dreams,
businesses which boom,
and most of all,
i'm being the best me.
doing it today
makes tomorrow limitless

it's just my reflection–
a beautiful face looking back,
me looking into those eyes
and seeing so much light,
all of it shining back to me.
it's a step up from before
when the mirror was dark,
the shadows caving in,
unable to breathe.
but now i see clearly
that it was all on me.
now i am a magnet
for everything i want.

brick by brick,
i knocked myself down
into sand on the floor—
no longer ready to be strong,
being told to be this way
time and time again.
i couldn't do it anymore.
but after i wiped the tears
one final time,
i was ready.
i rebuilt piece by piece,
stable and solid.
i no longer need him.
want him, yes,
but the desperation has vanished.
i will be stronger than ever.
this new version can take it.
now it's not being demanded of me.
i am here now—
an unstoppable force.

right now, i am so fed up,
feeling replaced though i don't want to be.
i want him to take me out, not her—
to spend his time with me, not her.
instead, i had to catch the bus
to come to a coffee shop
so i'm not waiting for him to be home.
this fucking sucks. today
i don't want it anymore—
to spend the nights alone,
not knowing where he is.
that used to be me he was with.
i should be the one he puts first.
it needs to be me he kisses.
i do not want this anymore
for i am done with it all.

i forgive you
for all the negative thoughts.
i forgive you
for thinking he doesn't care.
i forgive you
for sleeping with a friend.
i forgive you
for crashing a wedding.
i forgive you
for almost getting raped that night.
i forgive you
for throwing your life away.
i forgive you
for snooping time and time again.
i forgive you
for being shy sometimes.
i forgive you
for starting arguments.
i forgive you
for not trusting others.
i forgive you
for not believing in yourself.
i forgive you
for it all.

9 reasons you will never get over me:
i am always so passionate about the things i want.
i can be so messy.
i make the best lasagne.
i love to see the world with you.
i give you so much attention.
i show up in your dreams each night
i am kind to you even when you're moody.
i love to drink wine and can match your every swig.
i give the best cuddles when you snuggle into my boobs.

caroline, make the most of now.
drink too much wine,
enjoy all your moments together,
and kiss him multiple times a day.
caroline, use your mind.
don't think bad about him–
it's only a reflection anyway.
you need to do more on your own.
caroline, keep being creative.
don't stop writing,
and also, get your eyes tested.
step carefully when the radiator leaks.
caroline, use your credit card less.
you don't need all those courses.
focus more on yourself–
you have it all inside of you.

things i have done because i was lonely:
stood looking at van gogh in the dark,
got on the bus with love songs blasting,
stayed in bed for way too many hours,
had phone sex with the guy who claims to have a big dick,
got overly attached to a mediocre man,

missed you, missed you, missed you,

walked around the block in circles,
drunk too much shiraz in the house alone,
signed up for a dating app to swipe away the hours,
and sat in the cinema while pretending
you were in the empty seat.

the best mistake i ever made
in the heartbreak was sending an email
going on about a blow job
like it was the highlight of 17 years.
it was pretty good though,
so i'm glad i sent it.
it can remind you how good i am.

i want to be remembered as crazy and passionate,
not meak and mild.
that's why i reacted like i did
multiple times, but it hurt like hell.
i'd rather you think of me in that way
than dull as dishwater like your new one.
how fucking boring is that?

the world is ending and we're all going to die,
so i'm going to fuck him like crazy.
the world is ending and we're all going to die,
so i'm going to drink more sauvignon blanc.
the world is ending and we're all going to die,
so i'm going to laugh really hard.
the world is ending and we're all going to die,
so i'm going to eat too much pizza.
the world is ending and we're all going to die,
so i'm going to vegas to gamble it all away.
the world is ending and we're all going to die,
so i'm going to write, write, write.
the world is ending and we're all going to die,
so i'm going to swear like the potty mouth i actually am.
the world is ending and we're all going to die,
so i'm going to get him to fall madly in love with me.

you might think he likes you
but he loves only me.
he will never recreate
the connection we have with you.
it's time to move away.
find someone who is your match
because he is mine.
he will never hear that mix.
no matter how much you want to control him,
he only ever sees me.
he searches for me when he's with you.
he remembers me in everything you do,
so leave right now.
it's for the best.
i am the only woman he wants.
we will have happiness despite you.

i am the fucking prize.
i am irresistible each day.
i am unable to be replaced.
i am a proud writer.
i am living in a perfect body.
i am the richest person i know.
i am empowered and beautiful.
i am loved madly by him.
i am always the chosen one.
i am the fucking best.

i am getting it all today;
the sexy man on my arm,
the perfectly proportioned body,
the multiple book sales,
the successful businesses,
the fabulously decorated home—
they're all coming true,
that long list of dreams i have.
it's all orchestrated in my favour.
life is changing.
i no longer want to be mediocre
though i thought i was for many years.
i was not made to fall in line.

what i really wanted
when our legs pressed together
was for you to turn your head
look into every cell of me,
and kiss me like i am 21 again –
to devour my body
right there at the pub quiz
instead of answering questions about friends.
i wanted you to answer my needs,
to want me like you used to,
and get hard at my touch.
what a night we could have had
if only you said yes
to one final glass of house white.

no one knows what we're doing.
sitting across the table over brunch,
we look like a couple
and almost act like one.
to the world, we are together,
but behind the door,
it's different at the moment—
i know it won't be long.
when we can go to the cafe,
we hold hands and you smile at me.

when you look at me
like lindsey sees stevie
during that live landslide,
then i know we are back.
you used to do it.
i am ready again
i almost saw it in the car,
but it wasn't quite the right second.
the adoration will be here soon.

i like to sleep in my own suit now.
he could never forget me.
i'm discovering new but old songs.
i can't stand the taste of coffee.
i doubt myself almost every day.
there's a pile of clothes i'll never iron.
i don't always make the money i want.
he walked away but is still here.
that's right, all the rumours are true.

i'll be your only love–
how much do you love me?
i'll be your only lover–
are you hard now?
i'll be your only dream–
are you thinking of me?
i'll be your only woman–
are you proud of me?
i'll be your only fantasy–
how much do you want me?

it's only ever you.
it's only ever me.
it's only ever us.

MEET THE AUTHOR

Cleo Selena is a poet and writer living in
Yorkshire, England.

She loves to spend days exploring the world around her,
reading and enjoying an occasional glass of wine or two.

cleoselena.com
@lovewordsandwine